Crocodiles, Camels & Dugout Canoes

Eight Adventurous Episodes

by Bo Zaunders

illustrated by
Roxie Munro

Dutton Children's Books · New York

Till Donna Brooks, vår briljanta redaktör

—B.Z. & R.M.

The publisher gratefully acknowledges permission to reprint
short excerpts from the book *Full Tilt* by Dervla Murphy.
Copyright © 1965 by Dervla Murphy. Published by The Overlook Press,
2568 Rte. 212, Woodstock, NY 12498.

Library of Congress Cataloging-in-Publication Data

Zaunders, Bo.
Crocodiles, camels and dugout canoes: eight adventurous episodes/
by Bo Zaunders: illustrated by Roxie Munro.—1st ed.   p. cm.
Includes bibliographical references.
Summary: Presents eight adventurous episodes that took place
in British Guyana, Saudi Arabia, the Arctic, and other parts of the world.
ISBN 0-525-45858-1 (hc)
1. Adventure and adventurers—Juvenile literature.
[1. Adventure and adventurers.]   I. Munro, Roxie, ill.   II. Title.
G525.Z38   1998   910.4—dc21   98-10128   CIP   AC

Published in the United States 1998 by Dutton Children's Books,
a division of Penguin Putnam Books for Young Readers
375 Hudson Street, New York, New York 10014
Designed by Edward Miller
Printed in Hong Kong
First Edition
10 9 8 7 6 5 4 3 2 1

Contents

Preface

The idea for this book was born in the Sir Edmund Hillary Map Room at the Explorers Club in New York City. Roxie Munro, an artist (and my wife), was researching illustration possibilities for a book on libraries, and I was there with my camera, helping out. Surrounded as we were by thousands of maps, old charts, and an accumulation of globes, our conversation naturally turned to travel and exploration. Suddenly we were flooded with memories of expeditions we had read about from childhood on. Names cropped up chaotically—Magellan, Sir Francis Drake, Thor Heyerdahl, Cortés, Captain James Cook. Having grown up in Sweden, I knew little about such famous American explorers as Lewis and Clark. On the other hand, Roxie knew nothing of Sven Hedin, the Swedish explorer whose book *Pole to Pole* was once my bedtime favorite.

Realizing that we wanted to do a book on adventurous travelers and receiving the go-ahead from our editor, we began our research. We never presumed to undertake a comprehensive survey of travel adventure throughout history. Still, at an early point, we ambitiously thought we would cover each of the major continents and even contemplated going back in time to 1500 B.C. (after reading about Hatshepsut, an Egyptian queen who sent a seaborne expedition to the land of Punt in East Africa). Early travelers on our list included the Chinese explorer Hsüan-tsang (A.D. 602–664), Marco Polo (1254–1324), and Ibn Battutah, the fourteenth-century North African who, after some thirty years of journeying—from China and India all the way to Timbuktu—was considered the most traveled man on earth. Roxie thought it would be fun to illustrate Hsüan-tsang in a procession of thousands of elephants.

The problem with most of these ancient adventurers—although we may one day want to return to them—was the lack of sufficient source material. (This didn't apply to Marco Polo, who, for our purposes, suffered from overexposure.) We didn't want to speculate or guess at experiences. Whenever a story came to us in the adventurer's own words, it seemed livelier, more personal. We began looking for people who kept detailed diaries. We also decided against using the great explorers of the sixteenth and seventeenth centuries. They were professionals, often with conquest-driven agendas. Our interest lay in amateur explorers with a desire to see new places. The idea of opening each chapter with an exciting episode was triggered when I came upon Mary Kingsley's spirited account of how she fell into an animal trap while exploring West Africa.

For some time we thought we would include Peter the Great. Although well known for being the czar of Russia, it seemed he would add a fascinating angle to the book. Travel was his means of governing and bringing his vast empire into the modern world. Cocooned in his imperial sled, he would spend months traversing a wintry Russia. Reluctantly we gave him up. After all, how many people can be squeezed into an illustrated forty-eight-page book?

Besides, there are already several books about him—one of the reasons we also gave up on Charles Lindbergh, whose flight across the Atlantic seemed a possibility.

As we narrowed down our list of candidates—falling in love with some of them—we found that we had concentrated on the nineteenth and early twentieth centuries. This was a period in which the last unknown places on earth were being explored. Unfortunately, it was also an era of ruthless colonialist exploitation and domination of indigenous peoples—and nature as well. Technology, or the lack of it, came into the picture, too. A contemporary Charles Waterton, confronted with a live caiman, would be more likely to use a telephoto lens than a canoe mast and hunting knife to help document his find. And unlike today's astronauts, mountain climbers, and divers, most of whom work with a team and depend on sophisticated technical support, these adventurers were poorly equipped by our standards, with little but their wits and goodwill to shield them from a capricious and hostile environment. They also relied on the help of local crews, whose invaluable contributions often went ignored or underreported.

In the age of superhighways, jet engines, and satellite communication, is the kind of adventure presented here still possible? Our Irishwoman, Dervla Murphy, may have found the answer. Let your aspirations take you far, but travel slowly and close to the ground.

August Andrée

Dervla Murphy

Sir Richard Burton

Antoine de Saint-Exupéry

Charles Waterton

Mary Kingsley

Annie Smith Peck

N

W   E

S

Ernest Shackleton

CHARLES WATERTON

The eleven-foot caiman had taken the bait and was lashing furiously. The men shrank back in horror. But when one of them offered to shoot it, the expedition's leader, Charles Waterton, became incensed. As a taxidermist, his plan was to stuff this fearsome reptile, so there must be no bullet holes. What was to be done? Quickly, Waterton devised a scheme. He would use their canoe mast as a bayonet, thrusting it down the caiman's gullet. Minutes later, sensing that the animal was in "a state of fear and perturbation," he changed his mind. He jumped on its back, twisted its forelegs into a bridle, and rode it like a horse. Then the men grabbed the rope attached to the bait and dragged the strange steed and its rider ashore.

7

This bizarre adventure took place in 1820, on the banks of the Essequibo River in British Guiana (now Guyana), South America. "Should it be asked how I managed to keep my seat," Waterton later commented, "I would answer, I hunted some years with Lord Darlington's fox-hounds."

Born in 1782 into an English family prominent since the days of the Crusades in the twelfth century, Charles Waterton, the twenty-seventh Lord of Walton Hall in the county of Yorkshire, was an exceptional character in more ways than one. An amateur naturalist, passionate about the study of plants and animals, he was also a man who liked sleeping on bare boards with a block of wood for a pillow, and who thought nothing of suddenly scratching the back of his head with the big toe of his right foot or of clambering with apelike agility to "the top of a noble oak." Still, when a writer once called him "eccentric," he was deeply stung, declaring himself "the most commonplace of men."

His passion for animal life developed early. As a small boy, he roamed the splendid park surrounding his ancestral home, showing great proficiency in the art of finding birds' nests. Always eager to experiment and wanting to impress his younger sister, he once swallowed a lark's egg whole. After she told their mother, he was given "a mustard emetic." As a result, he could never afterward abide the taste of mustard.

This incident did little to curb the boy's taste for experimentation and bird study, however. At the age of eight, he was nearly killed trying to observe a starlings' nest on an unsafe roof.

When his first teacher, a priest and strict disciplinarian, thought frequent applications of a birch rod would change the unruly child, he sorely underestimated his charge. Priests at that time wore breeches and wool stockings, which were no protection against young Waterton, who in later years recalled how he "flew at the calf of the holy man's leg and made him remember the sharpness of my teeth."

Fortunately for him (and the priest), he was soon sent to a Catholic school where the teachers realized that there was no evil in the boy, only high spirits. To channel his energy, they made him the resident rat-catcher—a responsibility he carried out with great zest. The foxhunting with Lord Darlington occurred after he had finished his education and returned home. Riding to hounds was expected of the son of a rich landowner, but Waterton did it with such recklessness that his parents, painfully aware of their son's capacity for weird accidents, began fearing for his life. To keep him out of harm's way, they sent him to visit two uncles who lived in Malaga, in southern Spain.

Waterton spent over a year in Malaga. Unimpressed with Spain's magnificent cathedrals and art treasures, he roamed its countryside looking for birds. He began to write down his observations: "The red-legged partridges abounded . . . the vultures were remarkably large; whilst goldfinches appeared to be more common than sparrows in this country. During the evening, the quails and bee-eaters arrived in large numbers. . . ." He also managed to learn Spanish well enough to read and quote Spain's literary classic, *Don Quixote*, in the original. After returning briefly to England, Waterton left once again, this time for British Guiana, where his family owned several plantations. For the next few years Waterton managed these properties. Then, in 1812, he abandoned his life as a planter. Instead, he journeyed deep into Guiana's forests to obtain samples of the famous curare poison that the Indians used for their darts and arrows. Finding and analyzing this rare poison would be his contribution to biological science. This trip was also the first of four great travel adventures, later recounted in his book *Wanderings in South America*.

Not until he was well into his third "wandering" did Waterton ride the caiman—which followed his meeting with a ten-foot boa constrictor. Sighting this splendid serpent, he immediately wanted it for his collection of stuffed specimens. Since there was not a moment to be lost, he grabbed it by the tail. When the snake came at him, hissing angrily, "as if to ask me what business I had to take liberties with his tail," Waterton waited until its head was within two feet. Then, as he describes it himself, "I drove my fist, shielded by my hat, full in his jaws." The snake was stunned by the blow, and "I then allowed him to coil himself round my body, and marched off with him as my lawful prize. He pressed me hard, but not alarmingly so."

Waterton brought nearly two hundred creatures to England to be stuffed and displayed at Walton Hall. Soon he took a very different approach to wildlife preservation. To protect the wild birds (or "the feathered tribe," as he affectionately called them) against foxes, poachers, and other predators, he erected an eleven-foot-high wall around his estate. Waterton gave much of his income and much of his life to this project. When it was completed, in 1826, he had created the world's first bird sanctuary.

Not a shot was to be fired within these walls. As a defense against poachers, Waterton devised an elaborate system of decoys, which were placed strategically throughout the park. As a result, every time an intruder ventured over the wall and began shooting at what looked like a bird, the poacher more likely hit one of Waterton's contraptions. Infuriating as this might have been to the intruder, it made Waterton supremely happy.

When he was not traveling—he journeyed

across the United States in 1824, revisited South America in 1825, and made several trips to Rome—Waterton devoted himself to his bird sanctuary. He continually improved it, opened it up to the public, and was gladdened as more and more birds chose to make it their habitat.

Though he lived to be eighty-three, Waterton remained a schoolboy prankster at heart. As an octogenarian he once hid under the dining table when an old friend came visiting. He growled like a dog, then bit his guest on the leg, causing him to leap up in alarm. He also continued to climb tall trees barefooted, much to the astonishment of the growing numbers of park visitors.

Decades earlier, in one of his visits to Rome, he had challenged an old schoolmate to scale the facade of St. Peter's Basilica. Having reached the top and come back down, the two made their way to another monumental building, Castel Sant'Angelo, atop which stands a huge sculpture of a gilded angel. Waterton managed to climb onto its head. Still not satisfied, he balanced on it on one leg. Perhaps that is how he should be remembered—perched on one foot on the head of an angel.

RICHARD BURTON

Insatiable curiosity drove Richard Burton. As a Christian, he was forbidden to enter Medina and Mecca, the two most sacred sites in the Muslim world. So, to pass as a Muslim pilgrim, he studied the Koran, grew his hair long, darkened his skin with henna, and named himself "Shaykh Abdullah." If Muslims had discovered his disguise, he would probably have been killed. But Burton, the most noted and controversial traveler of the nineteenth century, was not only consumed with a desire for knowledge, he thrived on hardship and danger.

For six weeks, Burton explored Medina undiscovered, secretly jotting down everything he saw. Then he left for Mecca, joining a caravan that followed a hazardous inland route. The journey was grueling, but now—bathed, perfumed, and with his head shaved according to Muslim tradition—he stood at the gates of the holiest of holy cities, Mecca.

13

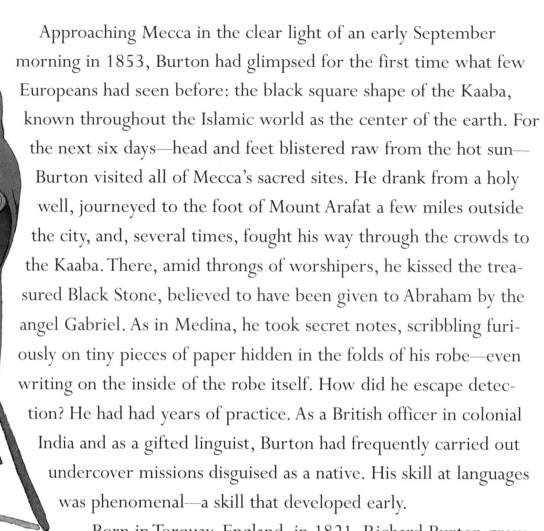

Approaching Mecca in the clear light of an early September morning in 1853, Burton had glimpsed for the first time what few Europeans had seen before: the black square shape of the Kaaba, known throughout the Islamic world as the center of the earth. For the next six days—head and feet blistered raw from the hot sun— Burton visited all of Mecca's sacred sites. He drank from a holy well, journeyed to the foot of Mount Arafat a few miles outside the city, and, several times, fought his way through the crowds to the Kaaba. There, amid throngs of worshipers, he kissed the treasured Black Stone, believed to have been given to Abraham by the angel Gabriel. As in Medina, he took secret notes, scribbling furiously on tiny pieces of paper hidden in the folds of his robe—even writing on the inside of the robe itself. How did he escape detection? He had had years of practice. As a British officer in colonial India and as a gifted linguist, Burton had frequently carried out undercover missions disguised as a native. His skill at languages was phenomenal—a skill that developed early.

Born in Torquay, England, in 1821, Richard Burton grew up in the French medieval city of Tours. His father was an English gentleman and a colonel in the British army. Richard began studying Latin when he was three years old and Greek when he was four. By eighteen, after living in France and Italy as well as England, he spoke six languages. Eventually he would speak twenty-nine, not counting dialects.

At nineteen, Burton went to Oxford. He was then growing a splendid mustache—fashionable on the Continent but unheard of at an English university. The moment he passed through the gates, a student laughed in his face. Stung to the core, the hot-tempered Burton immediately challenged the student to a duel with pistol or sword, a response that made him appear even more outlandish. Burton was never comfortable at Oxford. After two unhappy years he was expelled, not so much for having broken the rule against attending horse races as for having argued with his teachers that the rule ought to be changed. However, he could now join the army and travel to the East.

His quest for forbidden cities began with Medina and Mecca. Later he became the first European to penetrate the sacred city of Harar in East Africa. In Africa he also went in search of the source of the Nile—the great geographical puzzle of that period—and, instead, discovered Lake Tanganyika, the longest freshwater lake in the world. Traveling in West Africa, he explored Gabon, catching a glimpse of the gorilla—whose existence was in question at the time—and, like Mary Kingsley years later, investigated the cannibalistic Fang people. In Nigeria, he made a futile attempt to discourage the rampant slave-trading there.

Burton spent the last eighteen years of his life in Italy, writing copiously from one of the eleven desks he set up in his study to accommodate his many projects. He published over fifty books, on subjects ranging from swordsmanship to the Sufi cult, and produced a seventeen-volume translation of *Arabian Nights*.

More than anything, he was a traveler. He once wrote: "Of the gladdest moments in human life, methinks, is the departure upon a distant journey into unknown lands. Shaking off with one mighty effort the fetters of Habit, the leaden weight of Routine, the cloak of many Cares and the slavery of Home, one feels once more happy. . . ."

MARY KINGSLEY

"It is at these times you realize the blessing of a good thick skirt," said Mary Kingsley after she crashed into a cleverly concealed leopard pit, fifteen feet deep and lined with twelve-inch ivory spikes. "I should have been spiked to the bone, and done for," she explained. "Whereas . . . here I was with the fulness of my skirt tucked under me . . ."

The place was Equatorial West Africa, the year was 1895, and the spunky lady saved, thanks to her firm adherence to the dress code of the day, was a young Englishwoman who had come to Africa to collect species of fish and beetles for the British Museum.

17

Until the age of thirty, Mary Kingsley was strictly a dutiful daughter who nursed her invalid mother and rarely ventured outside her London home. Her father, on the other hand, as the personal physician to travel-minded aristocrats, was always wandering off to exotic places, from which he sent his family long, detailed letters about his adventures. When Mary was six and already doing household chores, such a letter arrived from the South Pacific. It contained a hair-raising account of how he had been shipwrecked on a coral reef near a cannibal-infested island. Included were descriptions of plant and animal life for "the learned one," as he called Mary.

Although she received no formal education—that was reserved for her younger brother, Charles—Mary had somehow learned to read, and loved nothing better than to lose herself in the books in her father's library. Science, travel, exploration, and piracy—subjects considered unsuitable for girls in Victorian days—were especially exciting to Mary. European exploration of Africa was reaching a high point in the second half of the nineteenth century, and much of what she read was current news. Dr. David Livingstone, who ventured farther into the unknown regions of Africa than had any other white man before him, was a favorite of Mary's. His respect and obvious love for the African peoples he wrote about made a strong impression on her.

From an inquisitive young girl—at one point she was granted permission to teach herself German, but only after she could starch and iron a shirt properly—Mary grew to be an unusual teenager. While still at home, she taught herself chemistry, experimented with gunpowder and electricity, and became engrossed by the intricacies of plumbing. Her favorite reading at this time was a periodical called *The English Mechanic*.

As the years passed, Mary became increasingly tied to her mother's bedside, rarely leaving it for more than an hour at a time. Then, in 1892, her father died unexpectedly; two months later, her mother also died. This was a terrible blow to Mary, but out of it came a sudden and powerful conviction: with the small inheritance left to her, she was now free to journey to the land of her childhood dreams—West Africa.

When Mary crashed into the leopard pit, in 1895, she was on her second visit to West Africa, traveling up the mighty Ogowe River in what was then French Congo (now Gabon). She was pressing her luck trying to get to know the notorious Fangs, reportedly a tribe of cannibals. This was part of what she called her "fish and fetish" mission. The fish were for the British Museum; the fetish referred to a study she was conducting of the region's religious beliefs and customs. Her father had been involved with such studies and, to Mary, this was a way of carrying on his work.

In search of the Fangs, Mary was traveling by dugout canoe with four native paddlers, pushing north toward yet another grand river, the Rembwe. At low tide, the waterways they followed became trails of stinking slime. They met with hippos and sandbanks. Once they were marooned in a crocodile-infested lagoon. When one of the reptiles tried to climb aboard, Mary was there with a paddle, ready to "fetch him a clip on the snout." Sometimes progress meant trekking through the heavy gloom of the rain forest. It was rough going, and the leopard-pit incident was just part of a day that had begun with a herd of charging elephants, continued with gorillas gamboling across their path, and included killing a snake as thick as a man's thigh. Later they cooked the snake for supper.

One evening, approaching a Fang village, they were suddenly confronted by a surge of tribesmen brandishing guns and knives. Fortunately, the village chief recognized one of the paddlers as an old friend.

The Fangs' dietary habits remained a mystery until, days later in another village, Mary noticed an unpleasant smell emanating from some small bags hanging in her guest hut. Pouring their contents into her hat, she found a human hand, four eyes, three big toes, and two ears—the remnants of what had once been a Fang dinner. Repugnant though this was, Mary took it in stride. She was later to discover many admirable qualities in the Fangs, such as courage and commitment to family.

After nearly a year of high adventure, Mary returned to England late in 1895, where she wrote about her experiences in a book called *Travels in West Africa,* published in 1897. It became an instant success, and she a sought-after lecturer and celebrity. In her public appearances she could be both serious and funny, peppering her narrative with plenty of jokes, often at her own expense. Mary was critical of the way the British colonialists had steamrolled their way into the African continent, with blatant disregard for its ancient cultures. In her lectures she was quick to voice her displeasure. In her second book, *West African Studies,* she combined research on tribal customs with her views on what should be Britain's political role in Africa.

In 1900 she sailed to Africa for the third time, but instead of going directly to her beloved "west coast," she responded to an urgent call for nurses in South Africa, where a war between British colonialists and Dutch settlers was under way. Assigned to a hospital in which the soldiers were dying by the hundreds from a raging epidemic, she became ill herself. She died two months later, and was buried at sea with military honor.

In *Travels in West Africa,* Mary remembered the Rembwe River. For three days her roost had been a bamboo platform at the stern of a roomy canoe with an old quilt for a sail. The captain, a big, friendly trader, was curled up at her feet, fast asleep after giving her the night watch: "Indeed, much as I have enjoyed life in Africa, I do not think I ever enjoyed it to the full as I did when dropping down the Rembwe. The great, black, winding river with a pathway in its midst where the moonlight struck it . . . Ah me! Give me a West African river and a canoe for sheer pleasure."

AUGUST ANDRÉE

*A*ttention! One, two, three, cut!"

The cutlasses rose and fell. The *Eagle,* released from its moorings, lifted majestically into the crisp Arctic air. Cheers and hurrahs came from the men in the shed below. The gas-filled balloon swerved dangerously, then rose, drifting over the icy waters of the Spitzbergen archipelago, some 450 miles from the North Pole. Clinging to the ropes of the gondola were the Swedish explorer August Andrée and his two companions, engineer Knut Fraenkel and physicist and photographer Nils Strindberg. Their goal: to be the first to travel across the North Pole in a balloon. The purpose: to make scientific observations. The date: July 11, 1897.

Two days later, a brief message scribbled by Andrée was picked up from one of the *Eagle*'s carrier pigeons. After that, nothing more was heard from the expedition for thirty-three years.

Salomon August Andrée was born in 1854 in Gränna, a small town in southern Sweden. The son of the local pharmacist, he was a strong-willed, independent boy who made his parents proud by winning many academic awards. At fifteen, Andrée felt that his high school classes were not leading to the "acquisition of useful and worthwhile knowledge," so he began attending the Stockholm Institute of Technology, where he graduated in 1874 with a degree in engineering. Two years later, he visited the Centennial World Exposition in Philadelphia. There, while working as a janitor to support himself, Andrée befriended a celebrated balloonist (ballooning was one of the exposition's great attractions). His new-found interest in the sport would grow to be a lifelong passion.

But Andrée had to make a living, and, back in Sweden, he went to work for the Royal Patent Office. In 1882, accompanying a Swedish scientific expedition to the island of Spitzbergen, he conducted, among other things, studies of atmospheric electricity. It was his first encounter with what he called "the white expanse of the north," and it may have been when the idea of using a balloon for polar exploration first occurred to him. As the years passed and Andrée advanced to chief engineer at the Patent Office, his dream of becoming a balloonist grew ever stronger. But balloons were expensive and hard to obtain. Eleven years went by before he was able to purchase one.

A patriotic man, Andrée named his balloon *Svea* ("Mother Sweden"), and with it he made nine ascents. During these flights he experimented with sails and draglines as possible means of steering; he took note of air currents, sound transmission, air quality, and other phenomena. Erik Nordenskiöld, discoverer of the Northeast Passage and the grand old man of polar exploration, asked Andrée whether a balloon might be used for making scientific observations in the Arctic. "Not only that," replied Andrée, "it could be used to fly across those icy seas all the way to the North Pole."

At a meeting of the Academy of Science in 1895, with Nordenskiöld's support, Andrée presented his plan for a balloon flight over the polar region. Even though some thought the project too risky—after all, a balloon only goes where the wind takes it, and once it's down, it can't take off again—Andrée showed such strength and conviction that within three weeks a balloon was ordered from Paris, and Andrée put together his team. Among the contributors were the Swedish king and Alfred Nobel, the inventor of dynamite and the founder of the Nobel prizes.

So, in July 1897, the *Eagle* was off. Almost at once, most of the draglines, which trailed the water's surface to steady the balloon at five hundred feet, came unhooked and fell into the sea below. Without them, the balloon rose to an altitude of more than a thousand feet. Andrée could have made an emergency landing by letting some of the hydrogen gas out of the balloon. Instead, he decided to push on.

Ahead lay fog, ice, and uncertainty. Still, the men experienced a strange feeling of lightheartedness. Although carried by the wind, they seemed in the midst of absolute stillness; even the Swedish flag hung limp. But below them, as they advanced north, the Earth appeared to be moving rapidly southward. If this speed kept up, they would be at the North Pole in no time at all. "How soon, I wonder, shall we have successors," wrote Andrée in his diary. "Shall we be thought mad or will our example be followed? I cannot deny but that all three of us are dominated by a feeling of pride."

Their euphoria was short-lived. Clouds and mist emerged, cooling the hydrogen gas and forcing the men to throw out most of the ballast in order to maintain altitude. On the third day, after they had flown sixty-five hours and were two-thirds of the distance to the Pole, ice coated the balloon, and it began to sink.

Andrée had no choice but to make a landing. The next morning he opened the valves to let the gas out, and the *Eagle* dropped slowly onto the frozen sea below. He and his men were now stranded in the snow-covered wastes of the Arctic Sea with no means of regaining flight.

How to get back to civilization? Freezing temperatures, fog, and high winds plagued the three Swedes as they trudged across the pack ice, each hauling a sledge with provisions salvaged from the *Eagle*. The tedium was broken when Andrée shot a polar bear—a joyful event, allowing them to feast on fresh meat. At first they headed for Franz Josef Land, north of Siberia. But then, as the pack ice began drifting in the opposite direction, they stopped walking and decided to drift with the ice. More bears were shot; Andrée wrote in his diary that "wandering butchers' shops" surrounded them. Finally, on October 5, they came ashore on White Island, a desolate, uninhabited piece of rock about fifty miles east of Spitzbergen. Here they made camp, planning to stay out the winter. . . .

Thirty-three years later, in the summer of 1930, a Norwegian sealing ship bound for Franz Josef Land made a brief stop at White Island. A few crew members rowed ashore and walked inland in search of drinking water. Near a tiny stream, they came upon an eerie sight: partially buried in the snow was a canvas boat loaded with equipment. Next to it, side by side, lay two skeletons, both fully clothed, one with Lapp moccasins on its feet. A short distance away, underneath a pile of stones, lay a third. Engraved on the tip of the boat hook were the words: "Andrée's Polarexp." The Norwegians had found Andrée's last camp. Among the items the crewmen brought back were Andrée's diaries, several rolls of exposed film, and—

a reminder of more optimistic days—some silk finery in the event that the expedition landed on Russian territory and gained an audience with the czar.

Remarkably, the film could be developed. In a series of stark black-and-white photographs, the saga of the long-lost trio sprang miraculously to life. Newspapers in Europe and North America carried the photos on their front pages. A wave of hero worship swept Scandinavia. Church bells tolled, torches and flares were lit, and over one hundred thousand mourners lined the quays when the remains of the three men were returned to Swedish soil.

For decades, the cause of death of the Andrée expedition remained a mystery. The men had fire, warm clothing, and plenty of meat, so it was unlikely that they died from exposure or starvation. In the 1950s, a Danish doctor read all of Andrée's diaries, paying careful attention to the symptoms Andrée described whenever the men fell ill: fever, cramps, diarrhea, muscular pains, and small boils. From those, and a mention by Andrée that they occasionally had eaten polar-bear meat raw, the doctor speculated that all three had suffered from trichinosis, a parasitic disease. So it is possible that the food that kept the men alive also finally killed them.

An even greater puzzle: What prompted Andrée, an intelligent and capable civil servant, to make an expedition that risked doom from the very beginning? And why did his action arouse such enthusiasm and hero worship? Asked about his decision at the outset, Andrée is said to have replied: "The task is so difficult that I cannot refrain from it."

ANNIE SMITH PECK

*P*oor little thing!" The people of Yungay, a town in the Peruvian Andes, clucked with commiseration as they watched the tiny, nearly sixty-year-old American lady prepare for yet another attack on the unscaled summit of Mount Huascarán. This was her sixth attempt in four years to climb what was said to be the highest mountain in the Western Hemisphere. Many of them had helped her gather food, a kerosene stove, climbing irons, and, not least, warm clothing.

Now, on this bitter cold August morning in 1908, Miss Annie Smith Peck was ready to face her formidable foe. Gray-haired, with steel-rimmed glasses, she was dressed in three layers of underwear, knickerbockers, two sweaters over a jacket, and four pairs of stockings. Finally, Miss Peck donned a ski mask—on which someone, rather incongruously, had painted a mustache.

Miss Peck, as she liked to call herself, was born into a prominent New England family in 1850. Her childhood appears to have been happy, even though, later on, her more conventional relatives disapproved of her academic career, her emancipated outlook on life, and her independent European travel. It was in Switzerland, on her premier trip abroad in 1885, that mountains first captured her imagination. Until then she had been a classical scholar and an archaeologist. She became ecstatic. "My allegiance previously given to the sea was transferred for all time to the mountains, the Matterhorn securing the first place in my affections," she declared. "On beholding this majestic, awe-inspiring peak, I felt that I should never be happy until I, too, should scale those frowning walls which have beckoned so many upwards, a few to their own destruction."

With the Matterhorn beckoning, Miss Peck started off by climbing smaller mountains, first in Europe, then in the United States. In 1895, she became the third woman in the nineteenth century to climb the Matterhorn. The feat made her famous, not least because she scaled the peak wearing pants instead of a full-length skirt. Miss Peck dismissed her own sudden fame as "unmerited notoriety," but welcomed it as an incentive to more important climbs.

Despite setbacks and extreme hardships, her passion for mountains never wavered. She would spend days, even weeks battling those "frowning walls" with the basic but primitive tools of her time: an ice ax, climbing irons, and a piece of rope. Sunburn, exhaustion, blisters, frostbite—all went with the challenge. She sometimes had to share her cramped tent with her guides and porters. But all that seemed to her inconsequential compared to the thrill of conquest, of beholding yet another magnificent vista.

Miss Peck's goal now, on this chilly morning in 1908, was the northern summit of the twin-peaked Mount Huascarán. To reach it, she and her men had to first scale the immense glacier that saddled the two peaks. As they worked their way up, a Peruvian porter lost his balance and fell into the crevice below, dropping the kerosene stove he was carrying. Dangling upside down on his rope, he was rescued by a Swiss guide, who also managed to retrieve the stove. A second guide proved less admirable. He first jeopardized the expedition by losing Miss Peck's mittens. Then, on their third day on the glacier, when they were almost to the top, he suggested they all rest briefly, only to use that time to sneak up to the summit himself.

Miss Peck was outraged. The guide had violated the most basic rule of mountaineering—that the expedition's leader be the first to step onto the peak. But there was no time for rebuke. In freezing cold and howling wind, she made it to the top herself, now worried about the approaching dark and whether they would ever get back alive.

The descent was a nightmarish ordeal down icy slopes, with just the moon to light the small steps they had hacked out on their way up. Miss Peck slipped several times, saved only by her rope. But they did make it. At nearly sixty, Miss Annie Smith Peck had conquered the "Apex of America," as she called it. "Oh, how I longed for a man with the pluck and determination to stand by me to the finish!" she often complained. However, as Amelia Earhart, the first woman to fly across the Atlantic, once said, "Miss Peck would make almost anyone appear soft!"

ERNEST SHACKLETON

The *Endurance* was sinking. As the crew of twenty-eight men watched in numb resignation from a nearby ice floe, ten million tons of ice were slowly and inexorably crushing her to death. Like a dying animal, the ship screeched and moaned as the pressure mounted. Finally her frames and planking broke with a sound that ripped like artillery fire through the frozen wilderness. It was October 27, 1915.

The men were the members of Ernest Shackleton's Trans-Antarctic Expedition. They had set out to be the first to make an overland crossing of the Antarctic continent. Now, before they had even reached land, they were stranded. They had salvaged three lifeboats, seventy dogs, and enough food for the next few months. But without the *Endurance,* Shackleton and his men were locked in an interminable jigsaw of ice floes, more than a thousand miles from the nearest outpost of humanity—and, since they had no radio, with no means of calling for help.

Almost a year earlier, after a brief stopover in South Georgia, a small island some 1,200 miles east of the tip of South America, the *Endurance* had sailed for Antarctica across the Weddell Sea. It had been a spectacularly bad season. Pack ice had begun accumulating almost from the beginning, first in narrow strips that the ship could circumvent, but then on an ever-increasing scale. When the expedition was only four hundred miles from the Antarctic coast, in late January 1915, the ice had closed so tightly around the *Endurance* that it could no longer move. From then on, there was little the men could do but monitor their drift with the currents and hope that the ice would break up. Below the Equator the seasons are reversed, so by March, winter had set in. To help his men cope with the unrelenting cold and darkness of the polar night—each year the sun disappears for 121 days—Shackleton had kept them occupied arranging hockey matches, dog derbies, parlor games, and lectures. He even encouraged them to carve out ornate dog kennels—or "dogloos," as they were called. Shackleton knew the value of keeping morale high and not giving in to despair and a sense of hopelessness.

Born in Ireland in 1874, into a middle-class Anglo-Irish family, Shackleton enlisted in the British Merchant Navy at sixteen. At twenty-seven, unhappy with the routine of Navy life and hungry for some great deed that would open the door to fame and fortune, he joined Robert F. Scott's expedition to Antarctica. Then, in 1907, Shackleton led his own expedition, the first to declare the South Pole its goal. When they were ninety-seven miles short of their destination, a food shortage forced Shackleton and his companions to turn back. Their return journey was a desperate race with death, in which Shackleton proved himself a superb leader. "He set men's souls on fire," as one man put it. Safely home, Shackleton was hailed as a hero and knighted by the king of England.

Now on this, his third expedition, the

ice had closed in, and the ship was gone. Shackleton called all hands together. They must haul the lifeboats to the open sea, he said, and then sail to South Georgia, the nearest inhabited island. It was imperative that they carry a minimum of weight. To make his point, Shackleton reached under his parka and took out a gold cigarette case and a handful of gold sovereigns and threw them away. He then astonished everyone by taking the Bible the queen had given him and laying it on the snow. The men were permitted to keep their diaries, but a two-pound limit was set on other personal gear. An exception was made for meteorologist Leonard Hussey's zither banjo, since a little music was considered good for morale.

Moving the camp across the jumbled ice proved impossible. The sleds, loaded with lifeboats and provisions, sank into the slush and snow and refused to budge. The men had no choice but to settle in for another long wait and hope that, by the time the ice had opened up sufficiently for the boats to be launched, their floe would have drifted close to some land.

They now lived in a world of unending wetness and inescapable cold. They would gather around a blubber stove and dream of pastries and vegetables. Adélie penguins showed up on their floating home and became their daily diet. Sometimes the men would catch leopard seals, a bigger and more dangerous game. Once, a twelve-foot seal chased one of the men across the ice and nearly ate him for lunch. The seal was shot, and fifty undigested fish were found in its stomach.

Months passed. Ocean Camp was renamed Patience Camp. On January 26, 1916, Shackleton wrote across an entire page of his diary: "Waiting Waiting Waiting."

As food ran out, the dogs had to be killed. Finally, in April, their ice floe had melted to the size of a football field. Shackleton ordered the boats launched. Fearing that neighboring floes would smash their small vessels to bits at any moment, the men scrambled for every available oar and rowed for their lives.

High waves rolled over the gunwales. Soon the men were knee-deep in freezing water. One day of misery followed another. No land, just swooping birds, endless stretches of ice and sea, and killer whales threatening to capsize their boats. Once, after they camped overnight on an ice floe, the floe split in half under a tent. One of the men plunged into the water below. Seconds before the gap closed with explosive force, Shackleton managed to pull him to safety.

After seven days on the open sea, the snow-capped peaks of Elephant Island loomed before them. A frozen rock some eight hundred miles from South Georgia, Elephant Island could hardly be described as hospitable. But to Shackleton and his men it was solid, unsinkable, blessed land, something they had not experienced for 496 days.

Camp was made on a tiny stretch of beach. For protection against the fierce winds, the two smaller boats were turned upside down and made into huts. Shackleton knew they would never be found in such a remote place. He decided to take their largest lifeboat and try to reach South Georgia, where a small community of whalers was running a whaling factory. For crew he chose some of his most quarrelsome men, in order to ease the strain on those he was leaving behind.

Ahead lay Drake Passage, a treacherous sea dreaded by all mariners. For seventeen days the men struggled with hurricane-level winds, fifty-foot waves, and the ever-present danger of iceberg collisions. Then, as they approached South Georgia, a sudden gale ripped off the boat's rudder, causing them to wash up on the uninhabited side of the island.

High, uncharted mountains now separated them from the whalers. Leaving behind three men too weak to continue, Shackleton and two others began a perilous climb across unknown territory. Several times they had to backtrack. Atop an ice ridge, they faced a choice between freezing to death or sliding down a steep slope that disappeared into a fog. Down they went, the wind shrieking in their ears, until they landed abruptly in a snowbank. Recalling the crossing later, Shackleton and his two companions confessed to the same strange experience: a curious feeling that a fourth person was with them all along.

On May 20, 1916, three ragged, filthy-looking men stumbled into the whaling factory. The manager could not believe that one of them was Ernest Shackleton. Like everyone else, he had assumed that the *Endurance* had been lost. Recognizing Shackleton's voice, he turned away and wept.

After a hot bath and a hearty meal—the first in nearly a year—Shackleton's party borrowed a boat to pick up the men on the other side of South Georgia. It took Shackleton three more months to rescue the crew on Elephant Island. Drake Passage thwarted him three times before he finally reached them.

From a small boat lowered from the rescue ship, he anxiously counted the men on the beach. All twenty-two were there, waving at him. The harrowing adventures of the Trans-Antarctic Expedition were over. The inspired leadership and sheer determination of Ernest Shackleton had triumphed.

ANTOINE DE SAINT-EXUPÉRY

*A*ntoine de Saint-Exupéry and his copilot braced themselves for certain death as their plane, shaking violently, plunged across the Sahara desert in the pitch-blackness of night. Miraculously, there was no explosion. Instead of landing on sand, the plane hit a small stretch of rounded black pebbles and rolled to a halt as if it were on ball bearings. Except for a few bruises, the two men were unharmed, but the plane's water container had burst. All that was left for their survival was a battered thermos of sweet coffee, half a bottle of wine, some crackers, and an orange. As dawn broke, the airmen looked for signs of life. They saw not a single blade of grass—just the emptiness of endless desert.

38

After camping in the plane for three nights, with daily excursions in desperate search of food and water, Saint-Exupéry and his copilot left the crash site and walked into the desert, hoping to find help. As they trudged across the sand, the unrelenting sun drained their strength. The light began to play tricks on them. What looked like an oasis would turn out to be just one more mirage. The intense heat dehydrated their bodies, and by dusk, their mouths were so inflamed that neither man could swallow. That night they nearly froze to death in the desert cold.

Then, on the following day, when they felt that only a miracle could save them, they were sighted by a small caravan of Bedouins. One knew how to revive them. Making them lie down, he gently unstuck their swollen lips with a feather. Then, to soothe their parched mouths, he rubbed mashed lentils into their gums. The delicate tissues, now badly infected, would have burst had water been given to the men too quickly.

The two pilots had crashed on December 30, 1935. In their attempt to fly from Paris to Saigon in record time, they had lost their way and run out of fuel. The idea of a pilot lost in the Sahara desert Saint-Exupéry later used in his book *The Little Prince*. It is an enchanting fable beloved by millions, in which a pilot meets a quaint visitor from a distant asteroid who tells him about the bizarre behavior of his neighbors in space.

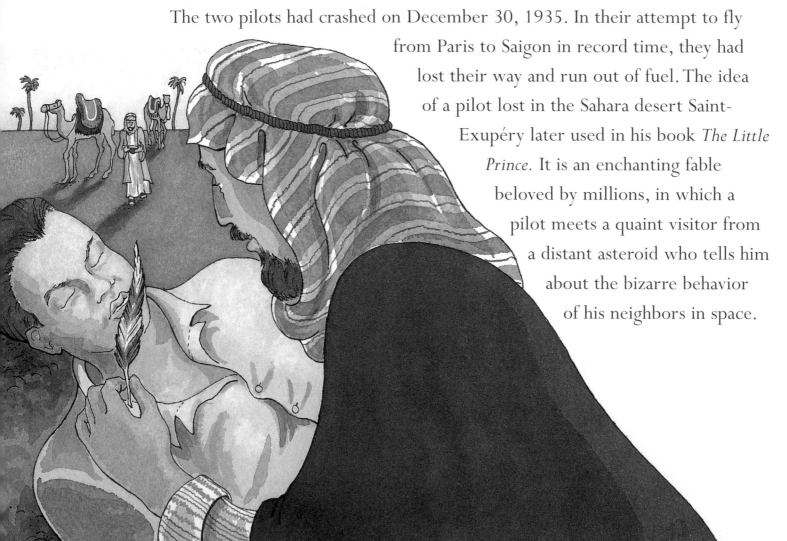

Born in Lyons, France, in 1900, Saint-Ex, as his friends called him, was a lively, unruly child. At age seven, he would ruthlessly wake up his sisters and brother in the middle of the night for dramatic readings of poetry he had just composed; at twelve, he tried to invent a flying bicycle; and at fourteen, he began his literary career by writing the autobiography of a top hat.

"Maman, if you only knew the irresistible thirst I have to fly," he once wrote to his mother. Coming of age in France, which at that time had more licensed pilots than the United States, England, and Germany combined, Saint-Ex was caught up in the fever of early flight. After he became a pilot, he was hired by Aeropostale, France's leading mail-carrying airline, and was sent first to North Africa and then to South America. Later, in his novels *Wind, Sand, and Stars* and *Night Flight*, he captured with precision and poetry the grandeur, danger, and isolation of pioneer flight.

When Saint-Ex wrote *The Little Prince,* in the early 1940s, he was temporarily living in New York City. World War II had broken out, and the Nazis had occupied his beloved France. Anxious to do his part, he eventually managed to enroll as a reconnaissance pilot at an Allied base in Algeria. From there he flew—with reckless disregard for his own life—several spy missions over occupied France. One day he did not return. Neither his plane nor his body was ever found. He was presumed dead, shot down by the Germans.

Part of Saint-Ex refused to grow up. When he lived in New York, he used to fill the sky outside his apartment with paper planes; he fashioned helicopters out of maple seeds and hairpins; and he once delighted in throwing water bombs out of a window overlooking Gramercy Park. What a pity it was, he felt, that so many adults lose touch with the wonder and magic of childhood. In the introduction to *The Little Prince* he writes with a tinge of sadness: "All grown-ups were once children— although few of them remember it."

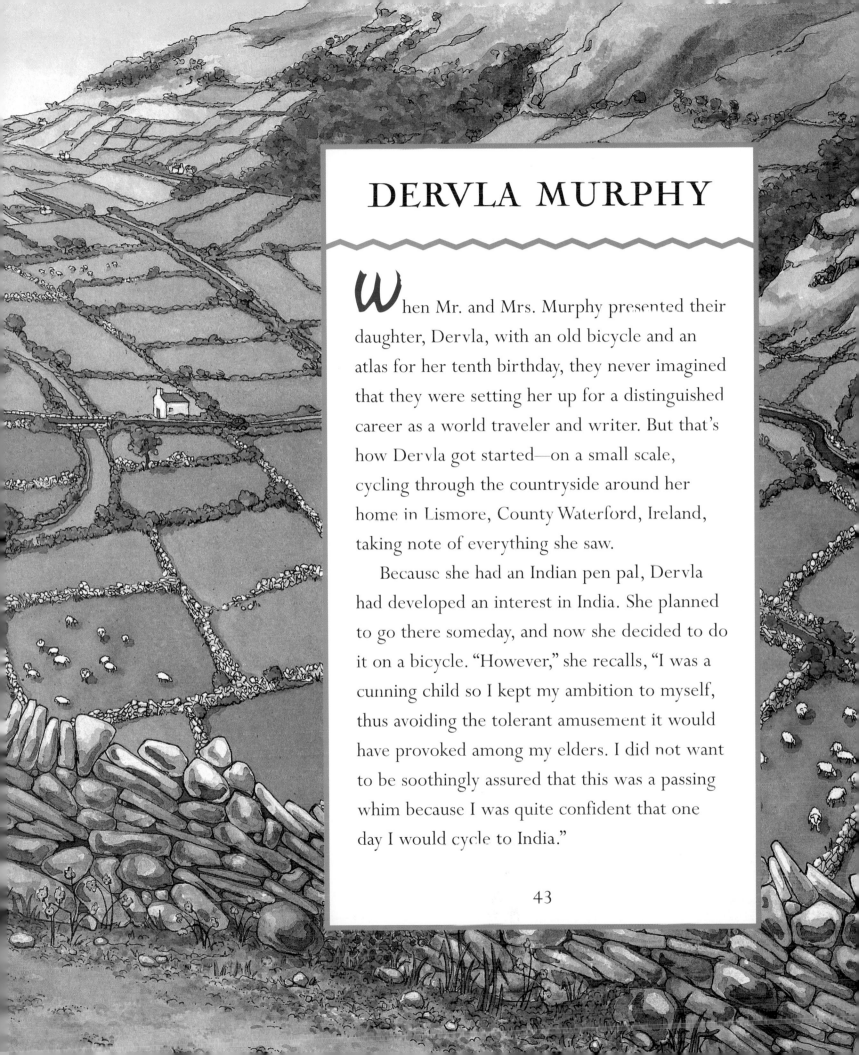

DERVLA MURPHY

When Mr. and Mrs. Murphy presented their daughter, Dervla, with an old bicycle and an atlas for her tenth birthday, they never imagined that they were setting her up for a distinguished career as a world traveler and writer. But that's how Dervla got started—on a small scale, cycling through the countryside around her home in Lismore, County Waterford, Ireland, taking note of everything she saw.

Because she had an Indian pen pal, Dervla had developed an interest in India. She planned to go there someday, and now she decided to do it on a bicycle. "However," she recalls, "I was a cunning child so I kept my ambition to myself, thus avoiding the tolerant amusement it would have provoked among my elders. I did not want to be soothingly assured that this was a passing whim because I was quite confident that one day I would cycle to India."

43

Dervla Murphy was born in 1931. When she was fourteen and still in convent school, arthritis began crippling her mother, Kathleen. As the only child, Dervla had to return home. For the next seventeen years, she kept house for her father, the county librarian, and cared for her sick mother. An avid reader, she educated herself by poring over the works of great writers, both classical and modern. Occasionally, when a friend or relative nursed Kathleen, Dervla was free to do what she loved best: take long bicycle rides, pedaling sixty or seventy miles a day. Once, in her early twenties, she cycled across Wales and southern England. Later she explored Belgium and twice rode through Spain. She always kept a detailed diary and, back in Lismore, turned her impressions into newspaper articles. In 1962 both her parents died. The following year, on a dark, icebound January morning in Dunkirk, France, Dervla saddled a man's bicycle she had named Rozinante ("Roz") in honor of Don Quixote's horse. Ahead lay France, Italy, Yugoslavia, Bulgaria, Turkey, Iran, Afghanistan, Pakistan, and—India!

The pannier-bags on either side of the back wheel carried twenty-eight pounds of clothes, medicine, toiletries, books, and spare parts for her bike. Also included were six notebooks, twelve pens, and a .25-caliber pistol with four rounds of ammunition. Although regarded by her friends as so much "adolescent melodrama," Dervla's purchase of the pistol would soon prove justified.

The European winter of 1963 turned out to be the coldest in eighty years, with temperatures often dropping to minus twenty degrees Celsius. Dervla thought it a "neat hell at the time," but also considered it "a reasonably fair exchange for the satisfaction of cycling all the way to India." She reached the Rouen youth hostel in western

France with a quarter-inch icicle firmly attached to her nose; in Grenoble, snowed-in roads regrettably forced her to take a train across the Alps to Turin; in the border town of Gorizia, Yugoslavia, she stood shivering for hours outside the warm offices of customs officials, trying to explain why she was so improbably entering the country with a bicycle in midwinter. It was in Yugoslavia, near Belgrade, that the need for the pistol became imperative.

Ice and piled-up snow had once more forced Dervla to get off her bike and temporarily travel by truck. Going up a twisting mountain road, the truck skidded and smashed into a very fortunately placed tree—beyond the tree was a sheer drop of several hundred feet. After ascertaining that neither she nor the driver was seriously injured, Dervla headed to the nearest village for help. On her way, in the deepening darkness of night, three wolves attacked her. As one hung by its teeth from the left shoulder of her windbreaker and another clung to her right ankle, she managed to slip off her glove, pull out the pistol, flick up the safety catch, and shoot them both. The third quickly disappeared.

Even though India was her final destination, it became less important to Dervla than the travel itself. Her book *Full Tilt* begins by quoting Robert Louis Stevenson: "I travel for travel's sake. The great affair is to move, to feel the needs and hitches of our life more nearly, to come down off the feather-bed of civilization and find the globe granite underfoot and strewn with cutting flints." As her journey continued through one country after another, Dervla took careful note of her mileage. "We only covered sixty-eight miles today," she would write, as if "Roz" were a friend.

On her arrival in Bulgaria, Dervla expected to find tangled masses of barbed wire and watchtowers manned by vigilant soldiers armed with binoculars and machine guns. Instead she saw a neat little bungalow, whose guard had left for lunch. She crossed the border, then returned a day later to get her passport stamped—passport stamps were the only souvenirs she could afford.

In Turkey, having finally escaped from snow and blizzards, she cycled in perfect weather around the base of Mount Ararat. Afterward she thought of this extraordinary mountain, where the Bible tells us that Noah landed with his ark, as a "personality encountered, rather than a landscape observed."

In Iran, the idea of a woman traveling alone was so foreign that people assumed Dervla was a man. She fostered that notion by cutting her hair short and by wearing army boots and a bulky army shirt. Thus taken for a boy, she slept once or twice in a barracks, surrounded by unsuspecting soldiers.

"The Afghan has not yet learned that tourists were invented to be fleeced," Dervla wrote in the ancient city of Herat. "Twice today my money was refused when I attempted to pay for tea. I am a guest of the country, so it pleases Allah when someone provides me with refreshment. . . ." Enchanted, she strolled through the bazaar, thinking that it couldn't have changed much in the two thousand years since Alexander the Great's soldiers had passed that way.

Dervla had been sorry to leave Iran and found leaving Afghanistan even more difficult. But then she fell in love with Pakistan, despite the hardships she endured there. Often hungry, she suffered heatstroke and cold blisters, was stung by a scorpion, and, during a riot over fares in a crowded city bus, had three ribs accidentally broken by a rifle butt. The mountainous region near Tibet tested her grit and her genius for improvisation when she could not ride but had to carry "Roz" across slippery glaciers. Facing a treacherous downhill, she decided to push her bicycle over, then half rolled, half tobogganed down the slope herself. "For a combination of beauty, danger, excitement and hardship (of the enjoyable variety), today wins at a canter," she wrote in her diary.

Six months after that icebound January morning in Dunkirk, Dervla arrived in India. Summer was at its height, so she abandoned her plans to explore until the weather cooled. While waiting, she looked for some useful work and found it in a refugee camp for Tibetan children.

In the mid-fifties the Chinese had marched into Tibet, destroying some six thousand monasteries and killing nearly a million people. Thousands, including the Dalai Lama, fled across the borders to India. Dervla, like many others, was particularly touched by the plight of the children. In the camp where she worked, in the Himalayan foothills, one doctor had to care for over a thousand poorly fed, disease-ridden youngsters. Dervla stayed there four months. In her diary, she wrote: "...when I left Ireland I was seeking only the satisfaction of adventure and discovery—but now, after spending the first half-year 'traveling hopefully,' I have realized that it is far better 'to arrive'...I am determined to return. . . ."

And she did. She explored India thoroughly and, a couple of years later, hiked—with a pocket pedometer—a thousand miles in the Ethiopian highlands. Since then, Dervla has traveled all over the globe, though not always on a bicycle, and written many books. In the 1970s she combined the roles of mother and traveler when she brought her five-year-old daughter, Rachel, along on a tour of South India. Five years later, the two trekked through the Peruvian Andes, following the ancient routes of the Incas.

At the time this text was written, Dervla was in London, arranging the rental of a good pack mule for an extended journey through Indonesia.

Bibliography

Charles Waterton 1782–1865
Aldington, Richard. *The Strange Life of Charles Waterton*. New York: Duell, Sloan and Pearce, 1949.
Waterton, Charles. *Wanderings in South America*. 1825. Reprint, New York: E. P. Dutton & Co., 1925.

Richard Burton 1821–1890
Burton, Sir Richard. *Personal Narrative of a Pilgrimage to Al-Madina and Meccah*. New York: Dover, 1964.
Rice, Edward. *Captain Sir Richard Francis Burton: The Secret Agent Who Made the Pilgrimage to Mecca, Discovered the Kama Sutra, and Brought the Arabian Nights to the West*. New York: Charles Scribner's Sons, 1990.
Simon, Charnan. *The World's Great Explorers: Richard Burton*. Chicago: Children's Press, 1991.
Viking, Byron Farwell. *Burton: A Biography of Sir Richard Francis Burton*. London: Longmans, Green & Co., 1963.

Mary Kingsley 1862–1900
Frank, Katherine. *A Voyager Out*. Boston: Houghton Mifflin, 1986.
Keay, John. *Explorers Extraordinary*. London: John Murray Publishers, 1985.
Kingsley, Mary. *Travels in West Africa*. London: Macmillan Publishers, 1897.

August Andrée 1854–1897
Andersson, Gunnar. *S A Andrée Hans följeslagare och hans polarfärd 1896–1897*. Utgiven av Svenska Sällskapet for Antropologi Och Geography. Stockholm: P A Norstedt & Söners Forlag, 1906.
Lundstrom, Sven. *Vår position är ej synnerligen god . . .* Stockholm: Carlsson Bokförlag, 1997.
Sundman, Per-Olof. *The Flight of the Eagle*. New York: Pantheon Books, 1970.

Annie Smith Peck 1850–1935
Olds, Elisabeth Fagg. *Women of the Four Winds*. Boston: Houghton Mifflin, 1985.
Peck, Annie Smith. *A Search for the Apex of America: High Mountain Climbing in Peru and Bolivia, Including the Conquest of Huascarán, with Some Observations on the Country and People Below*. New York: Dodd, Mead, 1911.
Tingling, Marion. *Women into the Unknown: A Sourcebook on Women Explorers and Travelers*. Westport, Conn: Greenwood Press, 1989.

Ernest Shackleton 1874–1922
Huntford, Roland. *Shackleton*. New York: Atheneum Publishers, 1986.
Lancing, Alfred. *Endurance: Shackleton's Incredible Voyage*. New York: Carroll & Graf Publishers, 1959.
Shackleton, Sir Ernest Henry. *South: The Story of Shackleton's Last Expedition, 1914–1917*. New York: Macmillan, 1920.

Antoine de Saint-Exupéry 1900–1944
Cate, Curtis. *Antoine de Saint-Exupéry: His Life & Times*. New York: G. P. Putnam's Sons, 1970.
Saint-Exupéry, Antoine de. *Airman's Odyssey*. New York: Harcourt, Brace & Co., 1942.
————. *The Little Prince*. New York: Harcourt, Brace & Co., 1943.
Schiff, Stacy. *Saint-Exupéry: A Biography*. New York: Alfred A. Knopf, 1994.

Dervla Murphy 1931–
Murphy, Dervla. *Full Tilt: Ireland to India with a Bicycle*. New York: E. P. Dutton & Co., 1965.
————. *Tibetan Foothold*. London: John Murray Publishers, 1966.
————. *Wheels Within Wheels: Unraveling an Irish Past*. London: John Murray Publishers, 1976.

OTHER BOOKS
Boorstin, Daniel J. *The Discoverers*. New York: Random House, 1983.
Courtauld, Augustine, ed. *From the Ends of the Earth*. New York: Oxford University Press, 1958.
Hagedorn, Hermann. *The Book of Courage*. Chicago: The John C. Winston Co., 1930.
Henriksson, Alf. *Antikens historier*. Stockholm: Bonniers, 1958.
Herrman, Paul. *Conquest by Man*. New York: Harper & Brothers, 1954.
Van Loon, Hendrik. *The Story of Mankind*. 1921. Enlarged Newbery Medal Edition, Boni & Liveright, 1924.